AUG 1989.

TO GILL,

MAY THIS LITTLE BOOK BRING YOU HAPPINESS.

Annette & Archie.

In the same series

The Coppice-Cutter, Trug-Maker and Besom-Maker

The Brickmakers, Farrier and Drystone-Dyker

The Harvesters, Milkman and Hop-Pickers

BESHLIE'S
COUNTRYSIDE

To Richard G.M. Cawthorne and Farrell C. Toombs

Published in association with

The National Trust
36 Queen Anne's Gate, London SW1 9AS

Text and illustrations copyright © Beshlie 1981, 1988
First published in Great Britain in 1988 by
ORCHARD BOOKS
10 Golden Square, London W1R 3AF
Orchard Books Australia
14 Mars Road, Lane Cove NSW 2066
Orchard Books Canada
20 Torbay Road, Markham, Ontario 23P 1G6
Published in association with Gallery Five
121 King Street, Hammersmith, London W6 9JG
1 85213 044 X
Typeset in Great Britain by P4 Graphics
Printed in Great Britain by Purnell Book Production

BESHLIE'S COUNTRYSIDE

THE BOOK OF

The Bodger, Thatcher & Rag-and-Bone Man

ORCHARD BOOKS

in association with The National Trust

London

Short-tailed Vole   Musk Mallow
Chamomile   Tricolour Pansy
Penny Royal

The Bodger

The Bodger was first in a line of several craftsmen whose work combined to make a chair. He began the process by buying a stand of wood, usually beech. Deep in this wood he made a simple thatched shelter where he lived, and rabbits and game were his for the catching. In the main picture he is splitting a butt — a chair-length section of a tree trunk — into *billets*. His dwelling is in the background.

When the trunk has been reduced to billets, he makes these even smaller by using

the *froe*. After this he uses a *side-axe* to trim the triangular sections into six-sided ones. He then sits on his shave-horse which grips the pieces, while he uses both hands on the *drawknife*.

Due to knots in the tree-trunk where branches had been, many billets were imperfect, and there was a great deal of wasted wood. So the word bodger came to be used for any craftsman who 'botched' a task. There are still inns called The Crooked Billet!

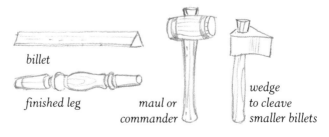

billet

finished leg

maul or commander

wedge to cleave smaller billets

10

To turn the billets into the familiar rounded *chairlegs*, the Bodger made a pole-lathe. He used a ten-foot springy sapling where it grew, tying a leather thong to the top, bending it over, and tying the other end of the thong to a small pedal-board fixed to a seat.

Bodger's froe

cutting edge

side-axe

The thong passed round the billet. When he pumped the pedal up and down, the thong spun the wood round. By holding a chisel to the wood, the leg was evenly turned.

drawknife for shaping

The Bodger sold his chairlegs to the Chairmaker. When all the suitable timber was used, he moved on to another wood.

Bank Vole   Purple Hairstreak
Wild Pink   Ivy-leaved Bell Flower
Cat's Tail Grass   Yorkshire Fog
Wood Millet

12

The Thatcher

At one time most roofs were thatched. Thatch is warm in winter and cool in summer. The pitch of thatched roofs is far steeper than any other and this assists the rain to run off.

The skilful craftsman once made use of all possible natural materials in his area. Bracken, heath, reeds, rushes, rye and hollow stemmed wheat have all been used.

Many consider the Norfolk reed to be the best and longest-lasting thatch. A good Thatcher can make straw resemble this, and

the result is called Devon thatch. Straw thatch is begun at the bottom of the roof and worked upwards to the ridge. Reed thatch is worked from right to left along the eaves, with the bundles of thatch overlapping.

tarred twine   *straw rope*   *wimble*   *twister*

All thatch must be securely fastened to the roof by passing *straw rope* round the roof rafters with a *needle*. This is then fastened to the thatch by *hazel spars*. In the main picture

needle

spar

the Thatcher is splitting a hazel stick
to make a spar. This is twisted in the
middle so that it forms a loop, and
the ends sharpened
to a point.

*yoke or
straw hod*

shears

Bundles of straw, called
yealms, are carried up the
ladder on a *yoke* or forked
stick. Uneven straw ends
are cut with the *shears*.

15

The thatch is combed with a *side-rake* to make the straw lie neatly and then beaten with a *leggat* so that it is even.

side-rake

hook

The Thatcher needs to exercise his greatest skill at the ridge-line of the roof. Reed will break here, so sedge or straw is used.

Pleasant patterns are made by criss-crossing the straw-rope at the ridge on the topmost layer of thatch.

trimmer

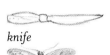

knife

Nesting birds can spoil a thatch, so birds and animals made of straw were fashioned and set on the gable to scare them away.

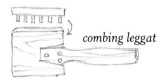

combing leggat

Shrew   Yellow Iris
Common Comfrey   Reed Canary Grass
Pellitory-of-the-Wall   Figure-of-Eight

The Rag-and-Bone Man

Rubbish was a luxury only the rich could afford. As soon as a cottager's property ended its life as one thing, it began again as something equally useful. For instance, a tin bowl with a hole in the bottom would begin a new life as a *sieve*, made by weaving wire across the open base.

The Rag-and-Bone man needed inducements when calling on countryfolk. First he rang his handbell to announce his arrival, then he offered small items, such as a *wick* for an oil-lamp, a *tallow candle* or a sacking-needle.

19

Up to modern times, some rag collectors offered gold-fish.

He wore a hat with a long flap. This protected his neck and shoulders from the rubbish he carried in a sack over his shoulders. In the main picture he has the empty sack in the basket and is ringing his bell.

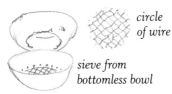

circle of wire

sieve from bottomless bowl

candle and wick

Country folk could not easily reach a shop, and every farm and cottage had a heap of useful rubbish. Markets were often a long way off so visits from itinerant tradesmen were welcomed. Everyone had to be inventive.

An old piece of *rusty water pipe* can be bent to form the handle of a *bow-saw*. The *tongue* of an old boot makes a fine *tap washer*. Old horseshoes, with the ends hammered out and pointed, make a sliding gate rail when put into fenceposts.

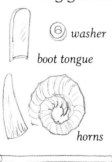

washer

boot tongue

horns

rusty water pipe

bow-saw

The Rag-and-Bone man pushed a little hand cart which he left outside narrow garden gates. He sold *bones* to the Gluemaker, and *cattle horns* to the Stick-maker, who carved them into handles.

bones